HANDY HOUSEHOLD TIPS

HANDY HOUSEHOLD TIPS

VIJAYA KUMAR

STERLING PAPERBACKS
An imprint of
Sterling Publishers (P) Ltd.
A-59, Okhla Industrial Area, Phase-II,
New Delhi-110020.
Tel: 26387070, 26386209; Fax: 91-11-26383788
E-mail: mail@sterlingpublishers.com
www.sterlingpublishers.com

Handy Household Tips
© 2006, Sterling Publishers Pvt. Ltd.
ISBN 978 81 207 5584 0
Reprint 2007, 2011, 2013

All rights are reserved.
No part of this publication may be reproduced, stored in a re
system or transmitted, in any form or by any means, mecha.
photocopying, recording or otherwise, without prior writt
permission of the original publisher.

Printed in India
Printed and Published by Sterling Publishers Pvt. Ltd.,
New Delhi-110 020.

Contents

1. Stains — 7
2. Cleaning — 23
3. Domestic Tips — 48
4. Sewing and Tailoring — 74
5. Gardening and Cut flowers — 76
6. Electrical Appliances — 79

Chapter One
Stains

Stains leave or make coloured patches or dirty marks on something. They can be an eyesore, and some are quite difficult to remove, especially if they are left for too long. Fingers can be stained with nicotine or the juice of some vegetable or fruit; a table cloth can be stained with gravy; children's clothes can be caked with mud, etc. Given below are some of the remedial measures that can be taken to remove particular stains.

Acid
- Treat an acid stain with a weak solution of washing soda, or a solution of ammonia, and sponge it off.
- Rub the area with a damp sponge. Mix a tablespoon of borax with half a litre of warm water. Work this well into the stain. Rinse with clean water and blot it dry with a dry cotton or with tissues.

Ballpoint ink
- Rub washing soap over the ink mark, and wipe with a wet cloth. Repeat this till the stain fades. Finally dab benzene on it and wipe it with a dry cloth.
- Rub methylated spirit over the area with a cloth. Wash in cold water and rinse as usual.
- Rub the ballpoint ink stain with alcohol, and wash with soap in lukewarm water.

- To remove tough ballpoint pen stains in a jiffy, dab the area with a little eau-de-cologne or nail polish remover.

Beer and Wine

Beer stains from your clothes can be removed by washing the clothes in warm water containing a few drops of vinegar, and then rinsing well.

- Wipe the wine-stained area of your dress with a piece of cloth dipped in soda water.
- Combine one measure of vinegar with five measures of warm water. Dip a sponge in this solution and sponge over the wine or beer-stained material. Rinse with cold water.
- Sprinkle salt over the wine-stained area, then steep in cold water for two minutes. Rinse as usual. For stubborn stains, use borax (1 tablespoon) mixed in half a litre of water.

Beetroot

Wet the stained area thoroughly. Rub washing liquid into the stain. Steep overnight in detergent solution. Wash as usual the next morning.

Betel-leaf

- To remove the stain caused by chewed betel leaf from clothes, use curd or lime on the stain.
- Wash the stained area repeatedly with a warm sugar solution, and then rinse off.
- To remove betel leaf stains from clothes, rub them with a cut guava.

Bird droppings

Remove the droppings, wipe the area with warm salted water. Steep overnight in detergent water. Wash as usual the next morning.

Blood
- Soak the stained cloth in salted cold water, for an hour. Wash with soap and water, and rinse well. Dry in the sun.
- Dried blood-stains can be removed by soaking the cloth in a quarter bucket of water to which one tablespoon of ammonia has been added.
- Add a tablespoon of hydrogen peroxide to a quarter bucket of cold water. Soak the blood-stained cloth in it overnight. Wash it the next day.

Buckets
To clean stain left by salt residue in buckets, wipe them with a cloth clipped in kerosene, and leave to dry in the sun for an hour. Wash them with detergent and water.

Candle spills
If candle wax falls on a cloth and leaves a mark, remove the wax, keep a blotting paper on the mark and run a hot iron over the paper. The stain will vanish.

Carbon paper
Carbon paper stains may be removed by sponging with methylated spirit.

Charcoal
Sponge the stained area with warm water, apply detergent powder, and keep aside for five minutes. Rub the area between your hands, and wash off with warm water.

Chewing gum
- To remove chewing gum from children's clothes, dab it with cotton wool moistened with eucalyptus oil. This dissolves the gum which will disappear.

- Apply an ice cube to the chewing gum to dry it up, then scrape it off.
- Apply egg white on the area. When dry, pick the chewing gum off the material.

Chocolate/Cocoa
- Wash the chocolate marks with plain soda water.
- Rub the stained fabric with a little borax powder, and soak it in cold water for a few minutes. Hold the stained area over a vessel and pour boiling water on the stain. Wash in cold water as usual.
- Rub the area with washing liquid, then steep in warm water to which a little detergent is added.
- Apply a paste of soap and limestone, and dry the cloth in hot sun. Wash the cloth as usual.

Coffee
- Dip the stained part of the cloth in glycerine overnight, and wash with soap and water the following day.
- Fresh coffee stains from clothes may be removed by sponging with borax solution.
- Dissolve soda bicarb in water. Soak the stained area in it for an hour. Rinse in clean water.
- If you spill coffee on your outfit while dining out, just wet a cloth napkin with a bubbling club soda, and sponge the spot.

Crayons
Rub with methylated spirit on the crayon stain, and wash off with cold water.

Curry

- Rub the stain with soap and place it in the sun to dry. As the stain takes on a pink hue, wash the cloth the usual way.
- Rub the stained part with a cut lemon, then dry it in sunlight for half an hour. Finally wash it off with soap and water.
- Rub with glycerine to loosen the stain, then rinse the cloth in warm water.
- Rub the stain with a grease solvent, then wash the garment in hot water and detergent.

Egg

- Egg stains can be removed by washing in cold water to which salt is added.
- Soak the stained cloth in ammonia water for 10 minutes, then rinse off in cold water.

Felt-tipped Pens/Sketch Pens

- To remove stains caused by a sketch pen, rub a little nail polish remover on the stain, and rub till the stain disappears.
- Dab the area with methylated spirit. After rinsing with cold water, wash as usual.

Fish

To remove yellow stains from your fingers after marinating fish, mix a teaspoon of lime juice with baking soda, and rub the mixture on your fingers.

Fruit/Vegetable

- To remove fruit stains from a coloured cloth, sponge them first with ammonia, then with petrol.

- Rub the affected area with paracetamol tablets, then wash off with soap water.
- To remove the dark stains left by bananas, cover the stain with glycerine, then keep aside for 15 minutes. Wash off with water and detergent power.
- Soak the fruit juice-stained cloth in a solution of borax and water, and then launder.
- Mix together one measure of hydrogen peroxide with six measures water. Steep the cloth in it for ten minutes, then rinse and wash.
- To remove stains due to vegetables, scrub them with the inner portion of a lemon peel or banana skin.
- To avoid stains left while cutting brinjals or raw bananas, apply a little oil on your fingers before cutting them.

Glue

- Dip a rag in pure vinegar and rub it over the glue stain on cloth. After a couple of minutes wash the cloth in sudsy water.
- If the glue stain is fresh, wash the garment in cold water immediately. If the glue has hardened, then use methylated spirit.

Grass

Green grass stains from clothes can be removed by sponging with methylated spirit before washing.

Hair Dye/Henna

- Mix together an equal quantity of ammonia and methylated spirit, and a little water. Dab this solution on the stained area. Repeat the dabbing process till the stain disappears.
- To remove henna stains, soak the stained portion in milk for half an hour, then wash with water.

- Steep the cloth in cold water. Rub the stained portion with washing liquid, then immerse in detergent and water solution. Keep changing the water until it is clean. Wash the cloth as usual.

Hard Water

To clean hard water stains on silk or jute clothes, rub with silver paper crushed and made into a ball.

Honey/Jam

- Soak in the honey or jam-stained cloth in detergent water that is warm. Rub thoroughly, rinse, and then dry.
- For stubborn stains, soak in a solution of half litre water and one tablespoon borax, rinse, and wash.

Ice-cream

- Sponge the stained area with a borax solution before washing the material.
- Ice-cream stains can be removed by using a grease solvent.

Ink

- To remove ink stains from clothes, keep the stained part immersed in milk for two hours. Then wash with soap and water.
- Apply salt on the ink-stained area, rub, and wipe it off. Wash the cloth with soap and water.
- Rub the stained area with a paste made of hydrogen peroxide and soda bicarb. Let it stand for four hours, then wash off.
- To remove ink stains from clothes rub the area with lime juice and salt for a couple of minutes, then wash them.
- Another way to remove ink stains is to apply toothpaste on both sides of the cloth, later washing off the paste.

- Wash the stained area with a solution of potassium permanganate or chlorine water.
- For fresh ink stains, apply talcum powder liberally over the stain. Wash.
- For an old ink stain, dab the area liberally with hot milk and lime juice. Let it stand for about 20 minutes. Then wash it off with soap and water.
- Make a thick solution with bleaching powder and water. Dip a small piece of cotton in it and rub the stained area with it.

Iodine

- Iodine stains can be removed by rubbing with a freshly cut lemon.
- Rub the iodine-stained area with a hot solution of soda bicarb.

Ketchup/Sauce

- Remove surplus ketchup with a cloth. Soak in cold water, then rub washing liquid into the stain, and wash as usual.
- Mix a teaspoon of glycerine in half a cup of warm water. With a sponge, clean the area with the solution, then wash.
- For stubborn stains, mix one measure hydrogen peroxide with six measures water. Soak the cloth for a few minutes, then rinse and wash.

Make-up

- Steep the garment with make-up marks in warm water containing a little ammonia, and then wash.
- Sprinkle talcum powder over the stain to absorb the grease in the make-up stain. Rub washing liquid into the stain, clean off with cold water, and wash as usual.

Mildew

- Rub the spots with soap mixed with powdered chalk. Dry in the sun.
- Make a paste of one teaspoon starch, two tablespoons salt and 1 teaspoon lemon juice. Spread this paste on the mildew spots, expose to sunlight, then wash well.
- For strong mildew stains, soak the affected part in alcohol for at least 12 hours, then wash.
- Lemon juice mixed with salt, and rubbed on the affected areas, is also useful in removing mildew stains.
- To remove light mildew stains from white fabrics, use a pinch of bleaching powder with a teaspoon of water to dab the spotted area, then wash.
- For old and persistent stains, potassium permanganate is effective.
- To remove slight mildew from clothes, dry the garment, sprinkle some salt and brush off.

Milk

- For a stubborn milk stain, soak the cloth in a solution of half litre water and one tablespoon borax.
- Sponge the area with club soda water.

Mud

- Soak the soiled cloth in the water in which potatoes have been boiled. Then rinse and wash.
- Scrape off the mud from the cloth, and then rub a slice of raw potato over the stained area. Wash as usual.
- Boil a handful of ivy leaves in half a litre of water. When cold, dip a sponge in it and sponge the affected area till the mud stain disappears.

Nail Polish

- Apply a dash of acetone on the stain and then wash in soap water.
- Apply white spirit on the back of the stain. Rinse and wash as usual.
- For a dried stain, soften it by rubbing some glycerine in it.
- Nail polish remover can also be used to remove a nail polish stain.

Newsprint

Dab the stained area with methylated spirit. Wash as usual.

Oil/Grease/Butter

- Old vegetable oil stains can be removed with petrol or benzene, and washed with soap.
- Place blotting papers over and beneath the oil stain. Press a hot iron over the blotting paper on top.
- Sprinkle talcum powder over oil stains on silk garments, and keep overnight. Next morning, dust the powder away.
- Eucalyptus oil can be dabbed on the oil stain, and after ten minutes, the cloth can be washed in cold water and detergent solution.
- Rub shikakai powder on a zari sari stain, and rinse with water.
- To remove oil stains from mirror or glass frames, smear the area with a little lime water, and allow it to dry. Wipe with a soft cloth, then with wet paper.
- Clean grease stains on pure silk saris with zaris by rubbing a cloth soaked in kerosene or turpentine, and wash off with soapnut (reetha). For imparting a shine, rub holy ash on the zari, brush it off with a very soft brush before ironing the sari.

- To remove oil stains from woollen garments, apply a little curd over the area, and wash.
- For removing grease stains from clothes, rub gram flour (besan) on the spot. Keep the cloth in the sun for half an hour before washing it.
- To remove grease from a terylene or nylon fabric, cover the stain with chalk or talcum powder, and then wash with soap and water.
- To remove car grease, sponge with cleaning petrol or benzene.
- To remove grease from your hand, place a dab of shaving cream on one hand, and sprinkle some sugar on the other. Rub your hands together and rinse well.
- Greasy coat collars can be sparkling clean if they are rubbed with a soft rag dipped in ammonia.
- For butter stains, scrape away as much butter as possible. Then rub the stain with a small amount of washing liquid. Sponge off with warm water.

Lipstick

- To remove lipstick stains from a washable fabric, apply glycerine on the stain. Let it stand for half an hour or more, then wash with soap and water.
- Apply acetone or nail polish remover on the stained spot, and then wash in soapy water.
- Rub petroleum jelly into the stain, clean off with warm water. Wash as usual.
- Dab a little methylated spirit on to the stain, then glycerine and rub lightly. Clean off with warm water, and wash.

Garments

- For stains on white silks, smear them with a paste of soda bicarb and water. Leave it in the sun for 10 minutes. Rinse in cold water.

- Lightly brush the stains on silk saris with eucalyptus oil, and wipe with tissues or a soft cloth.

Embroidery Mark

Embroidery trace marks can be removed if wiped with a piece of cotton wad dipped in methylated spirit.

Paint

- If the paint on the garment is fresh, place a blotter on top of the stain and run a warm iron over it.
- Rub petroleum jelly into the stain. Then wash thoroughly, using plenty of soap and water.
- Dab methylated spirit on stains of emulsion paint before washing.
- Turpentine can be used instead of methylated spirit to remove emulsion paint stains.

Pencil

- Stains of indelible pencil can be removed by rubbing the spot with methylated spirit.
- Dark and persistent pencil marks can be removed by soaking the stained spot in alcohol.

Perfume

- Treat perfume stains with dilute hydrogen peroxide. Then wash with soap and water.
- Rub in glycerine diluted in warm water, then wash.

Perspiration

- When only the collar of a coat or shirt is dirty, rub it with powdered magnesia, and brush off.
- To remove perspiration odour and stains from woollens, sponge the area with lemon juice and water, and hang in the sun.

- Soak the sweat-stained clothes in water containing three tablets of aspirin.
- Before washing the stained clothes, sponge the area with weak vinegar or ammonia.

Rust

- Rinse the iron-stained clothes in hot water. Then rub a cut lime over the stains, and wash with soap and boiling water.
- To remove rust stains from garments, apply thick calcium carbonate solution to the stained area, and keep aside for an hour. Rub with an old toothbrush, and wash with cold water.
- To remove iron mould on white linen and cotton, soak in household bleach for an hour. Wash as usual.
- If there are shiny iron marks on a dress, place a newspaper over the area and press with a warm iron.
- To remove iron mould on your white fabrics, cover the stain with salt and lime juice, and leave it in the sun for an hour before washing.
- For rust marks on cotton on linen, soak the cloth in day-old rice water, which will remove the most stubborn spot.

Scorch

- If you have scorch stains on your clothes, sprinkle the spot with hydrogen peroxide, place a white cloth over the mark, and iron.
- Rub washing soap on the stain until a thick layer is formed. Keep in the sun for an hour, then wash.
- Rub washing liquid into the scorch mark. Dab with a solution of one tablespoon of borax with half a litre of warm water, then wash as usual.

- A light scorch mark can be removed by soaking the area in cold milk as soon as possible.
- Mix one tablespoon of bleach in one litre of water. Soak the scorched material in it for an hour. Then rinse.

Shoe Polish
- To remove shoe polish stain, rub it with methylated spirit and then finally rinse in hot water.
- Apply eucalyptus oil with a clean pad of soft cloth on the stain on a silk material. Sponge with lukewarm water later.
- Sooty spots can be removed by washing the affected parts with hot soap suds.

Tar
- Place the tarred area of the cloth in a saucer. Pour pure olive oil over it and let it soak overnight. Wash in water as usual the next day.
- Scrape off as much of the tar as you can. Sponge the area with benzene or eucalyptus oil. Wash in warm soapy water.
- To remove tar from the hands, rub the hands with the peel of a fresh lime or orange, then wash off with tepid water.
- Rub the stained area with a little kerosene till the stain disappears. Wash the cloth with detergent and water.
- Remove the tar stain with a grease solvent, and rinse in warm water.
- Scrape away surplus tar, then soften the remaining tar with glycerine rubbed into it. Rub eucalyptus oil from the back of the stain, and wash in hot water.

Tarnish
Remove tarnish from gold and silver thread fabrics by rubbing gently with a cloth dampened in liquid ammonia.

Tea

- Dip the stained part in glycerine overnight. Wash with soap and water the next day.
- Tea stains on a white cloth can be removed by rubbing sugar into it.
- For old tea stains, steep the garment in a hot solution of borax and water. When the mixture cools, rinse and wash.
- Rub the stain with ammonia solution, and then wash with soap and water.
- To remove tea stains from clothes, wash them with a solution of salt and lemon juice.
- If you spill tea over a tablecloth or bedsheet, sprinkle some talcum powder over the area. After 20 minutes, remove the powder, and wash the cloth.
- Potassium permanganate removes older stains. Rub the chemical into the stain, and wash the cloth in cold water.
- To get rid of tea stains, soak your china in a solution of bleaching powder and water. Rinse off with soap solution in the morning.

Tobacco

Tobacco stains may be removed by rubbing with lemon juice and pumice stone.

Urine

- To remove stubborn urine stains from your clothes, sponge with mild ammonia or soda bicarb. Rinse well and wash.
- Mix one measure of hydrogen peroxide with six measures of cold water. Steep the cloth in it for a few minutes, then wash in very hot water.

Varnish

Dab with methylated spirit. Then wash with soap and water.

Vinegar

- Vinegar stains on your clothes can be removed by sponging with one teaspoon of ammonia mixed in half a litre of water.
- Rub the area with a damp sponge. Mix together one tablespoon of borax with half a litre of water. Work this well into the stain. Rinse in clean water.

Chapter Two
Cleaning

You can bring back the shine to your old, dull and drab-looking articles by cleaning. Not only do you economise on things by cleaning at home, it also gives you immense satisfaction to achieve something for yourself. So start using the following tips today.

Aluminium Vessels
To clean the burnt stains from an aluminium vessel, rub it with sandpaper.

Bags/Purses
- To clean leather and foam leather bags or purses, use cotton soaked in kerosene. Dry the article under the sun, then polish it with mustard or coconut oil to get a shine.
- The zips of purses and bags will slide easily if you rub a candle over them.
- To clean fungus spots off your leather purse, rub it all over with a candle, and shine it with a soft cloth.

Bolts/Nuts/Nails
- Shine the bolts and handles on doors with lemon juice and turpentine oil every fortnight, and you will see the difference.

- Run a pencil over door locks and hinges, for efficient working.
- If you are stuck with a key that will not turn easily in a lock, rub a pencil along the jagged edge. The graphite in the pencil makes it easier to turn the key.
- In order to avoid the plaster of the wall coming off while nailing, immerse nails in warm water before nailing them into the wall.
- A drop of ammonia will loosen up a rusty screw that is difficult to extract.
- Keep spare nails and screws free of rust by spraying them with light oil.
- To avoid nails getting bent while hammering them into a wall, coat the nail with any oil, tap three-four times the area where the nail is to be put, and then hammer it in with ease.
- Store nails, nuts and bolts in Vaseline bottles or cream containers to prevent them from rusting.
- If you find it difficult to hammer a nail into any wooden surface, then first drive the nail into a bar of soap.
- To avoid iron tools becoming rusty in a box, keep some camphor inside the tool box.

Books

- In order to clean soiled edges of books, erase with very fine sandpaper or a soft eraser.
- While dusting books regularly, use a soft brush instead of a cloth.
- To preserve the condition of valuable manuscripts and books from insects and termites, keep a few pieces of sandalwood in the bookcase.
- Keep a few dried leaves of neem inside books to keep away insects and silver fish.

- When your child's notebook becomes dirty due to constant erasures, clean it with a piece of bread.

Bottles/Jars

- If bottles are dirty from inside, add some water and skins from boiled potatoes. Shake the bottles well, then rinse them with clean water.
- For small-necked bottles into which you can't fit a bottle-brush, mix two tablespoons of raw rice in one-fourth cup of vinegar, pour into the bottles, shake well and rinse.
- To clean a narrow-mouthed bottle, put a little toothpowder in it, add warm water, shake vigorously, and then clean with clear water.
- Used tea leaves and crushed egg shells act as abrasives for cleaning narrow-necked bottles.
- To clean narrow-mouthed bottles without using a brush, put some rice grains, detergent and water in them. Shake vigorously, and clean with clear water.

Brassware

- To clean your brassware and make them shine, boil water with a little onion in it. Wash your brassware with it.
- Sprinkle a few drops of kerosene on a cloth and wipe the brassware that has been cleaned with metal polish, to give it that extra shine for a longer.
- Scrub your brassware vigorously with dry ash, then wipe with a piece of newspaper. This will give your brassware a shiny finish.
- To polish brass, add cooking vinegar to fine clean brassware, scrub them with a handful of hibiscus leaves and salt.
- Cut an orange in half. Dip the cut surface in a mixture of fine ash and salt, and rub this over your brassware.

- Add a few drops of mustard oil to turmeric powder. Rub your brassware with this to give it a shine.
- Collect lemon peels that have recently been squeezed. Rub the brassware with these. Wipe with a clean muslin cloth to get your brassware shining.
- Clean your brassware with lemon and salt before using brasso on them. This speeds up the process of shining, as well as economises on the use of brasso.
- To make brass objects retain their brightness for a longer period, wash with a mixture of finely powdered brick and seedless tamarind, wash in water and immediately polish dry with a soft cloth.
- Mix two tablespoons of vinegar with a little less of cleaning powder. Clean your brassware with this mixture, using a dry napkin. Let it stand for sometime, then wash and dry well.
- After polishing your brassware, brush the surface with a coat of colourless nail polish for the brassware to retain their shine for a long time.
- Add a few drops of three-in-one sewing machine oil to a little turmeric powder. Use this to clean and give a shine to your brassware.
- To remove dirt and stains from your brassware, rub with salt that is moistened with a little vinegar.
- For tarnished brass, rub with the rind of a lemon.

Brushes/Combs
- Dissolve half a tablespoon of washing soda in some warm water. Dip the bristles in it, ensuring that the roots don't get wet. Stand the brush on its bristles to dry, away from direct heat. To dislodge grime from between the bristles, use a toothpick.

- To clean a shoe brush, stand it, bristles downwards, in some white spirit. Pat the brush up and down in the spirit, then stand it on a thick newspaper to drain. Rinse with water and soap. Then dry again.
- After using the brush for distempering, wash it in hot water, wipe it and dry away from heat.

Car Wipers
- For smooth movement of car wipers, rub the windscreen with a piece of soap.
- If your car wipers do not work, rub a half-cut potato on the windscreen. Rain water will not stay on it.

Carpets
- Before brushing your carpet, sprinkle salt over it and let it stand for ten minutes. The grime and dust come out faster.
- Sprinkle your carpets or dhurries with used tea leaves. Then sweep them. The dust will stick to the tea leaves and not settle elsewhere.
- To remove dirt from a coir carpet, spread baking soda on its surface, and brush the surface after 15 minutes. The dirt gets removed on brushing, and the soda leaves the carpet glistening.
- For cleaning carpets at home, add two tablespoons of ammonia to one litre of water. Dampen some saw dust with this solution, and scatter over the dirty carpet, brushing gently in all directions. Leave it to dry. Brush away the saw dust into a dustpan.
- Carpet which has been flattened due to something being placed on it can be revived by leaving an ice cube on the spot overnight. Dry the carpet the following day.
- To remove hair from a carpet, wipe with a sponge dampened with white vinegar and water.

- To clean a stain on your carpet, rub a cut potato over it. When dry, rub with a soft brush.

Chinaware/Ceramics

- To prevent dust or stains accumulating on cracks in your chinaware or ceramics, apply a coat of clear nail polish on the cracks.
- To retain the lustre on your china or ceramics, wash them with baking soda.
- Apply a little furniture wax to the insides of ashtrays to ensure ash does not cake the trays.
- To remove tea or coffee stains from china, dip a soft cloth in common salt and clean the chinaware.
- Burnt marks from ceramics can be removed by rubbing the spots with a mixture of vinegar and salts.

Crockery

- In order to remove the smell from crockery, rub the dishes with used tea leaves, or rinse with a little vinegar.
- To clean plates, sprinkle some salt on them, add a little hot water, and leave as it is till the water cools. Then rinse the plates.

Curtains

- Clean the build-up of soap on a shower curtain by soaking the curtains in warm water with a little salt added to it. This prevents mildew appearing on it.
- Fold net curtains into squares, and leave to soak overnight in warm soapy water. Rinse, gently squeeze out surplus water and spread them out flat to dry.

Doors/Windows/Gates

- Clean your window glasses with a solution of soda bicarb and water.

- The glasses of doors and windows can be cleaned by rubbing with a mixture of lime and glycerine.
- To clean metal door handles, dampen cloth in nail polish remover, and rub. This gives a sparkling shine.
- Give your window panes and glass doors sparkle and shine. Chop nine to ten small onions. Boil them in one litre of water. When cool, remove the onion pieces, dip a sponge into the water after adding a teaspoon of detergent to the water. Scrub the glass, and leave for a minute. Wash with clear water.
- To get your windows shining, polish with a wad of damp newspapers, then with dry ones.
- To stop windows misting up, wipe them with a cloth dipped in methylated spirit and glycerine solution.
- Scrub the wrought iron gates thoroughly with a wire brush and emery paper. Apply a coat of metal primer before applying two exterior coats of enamel paint.
- Remove the dirt on hinges of your door with a toothbrush, then dab with Vaseline or machine oil to avoid the door creaking.
- Add ammonia, white vinegar and two tablespoons of cornflour to a bucket of water. Wash your windows with this solution, then dry with a newspaper.
- For greasy windows, wash with a tablespoon of starch diluted in a litre of water.

Drains/Sinks/Taps

- To clean drains and keep them odour-free, throw in a handful of baking soda in them, following it with hot water.
- Add caustic soda to water and boil. Pour this into the drain to remove any clogging.

- To clear a choked drain, pour a cup of baking soda down the drain, followed by a cup of vinegar. As it foams, run hot water down the drain, followed by a cup of vinegar. As it foams, run hot water down the drain.
- To keep the wash basin sparkling, sprinkle a bit of ultramarine on the basin and rub well. Wash off after five minutes, rubbing well.
- To keep the drain pipe of your kitchen sink free of any blockage, pour the leftover hot water from the pressure cooker into it daily.
- Use a solution of salt and turpentine to whiten your wash basins.
- Use milk packets as scrubbers to clean sinks. The result is simply great!
- To remove the rust stains from taps, rub with vinegar.
- If you have accidentally poured hot fat down the sink, immediately pour a pan of very hot water down it to avoid the fat solidifying and thus creating a blockage.
- Remove hard stains on sinks by rubbing vinegar on the mark.

Flasks

- To clean flasks and remove strange smells from unused flasks, put half a cup of vinegar, let it stand for some time, then wash with cold water.
- To clean a flask, crush an eggshell and drop it into the flask, adding some hot water. Shake the flask, then leave it overnight to soak. Rinse thoroughly the following day.
- To remove the persistent smell of tea or coffee lingering on in a flask, put two tablespoons of soda bicarb and a large cup of boiling water. Shake well and leave for 10 minutes. Then rinse well with boiling water, and dry.

Floors

- Instead of phenyle, put two teaspoons of salt in a bucket of water, and use this for swabbing floors.
- Stitch together old socks to make a mop. Wiping your floors with this will give a better effect as socks absorb dirt better.
- To clean floors, add a little white phenyle and a tablespoon of kerosene oil to half a bucket of water. The solution not only makes the tiles shine better, but also keeps away mosquitoes and ants.
- If you drop an egg on the floor, spread a little salt over it and leave it for 15 minutes. Then clean it with a mop.
- When oil spills on the floor, sprinkle some rice flour, or wheat flour, or gram flour. Wipe it with a newspaper first, then clean it with a wet mop.
- When you put kerosene in water and use this solution for mopping, add 12 drops of lavender and two tablespoons of vinegar to avoid the smell of kerosene.
- To clean the white stains left by lime juice, rub the area with the core of a cucumber or pumpkin.
- Stone floors are best cleaned with water containing a small amount of washing soda.
- After using a floor mop, rinse it thoroughly in a bucket of water to which is added several drops of household disinfectant to kill off any lingering bacteria which might be present.

Framed Pictures

Dab some eau-de-cologne on a piece of cloth, and wipe the glass of the framed picture to remove all traces of spots and grease or dust.

Furniture

- Sprinkle talcum powder or gram flour on oil-stained glass table tops, and rub with a dry towel.
- Use a piece of flannel dampened with petrol to clean the soiled arms of chairs.
- To remove water stains from waxed surface of furniture, pour liquid wax over it and wipe off immediately. Renew surface finish with fresh wax.
- To remove crayon marks from table surfaces, rub a little kerosene or cigaratte ash on them, then clean with a cloth.
- Dip a clean cloth in liquid paraffin. Squeeze out the liquid and leave to dry. Use this cloth to dust the furniture, for it picks up dirt much better than ordinary cloth.
- To darken wooden furniture, apply a coat of beer. Let it dry, then apply polish.
- Clean your mahogany furniture with a cloth dipped in cold tea before polishing to give it that extra rich colour.
- To keep wooden furniture new, add a teaspoon of turpentine and three tablespoons of linseed oil to one and a half litres of boiling water. When cold, apply it on the furniture like any other polish.
- To remove white marks from furniture, dampen a cloth in vinegar, dab it in cigarette ash, and then rub firmly over the marks.
- Use boiled linseed oil to polish walnut wood furniture.
- To make your wickerwork furniture look much cleaner and brighter, wash it first with soap and water, then with a solution of salt and water.
- Clean bamboo and cane furniture with salted water.
- To remove dirt on new furniture rub used tea leaves on it, and clean it off with a dry cloth.

- If cane chairs are very discoloured, try rubbing over with a cut lemon, or wash in hot water to which lemon juice has been added.
- Rub walnut furniture with a cloth dampened with liquid paraffin, and then polish in the usual way.
- To get a good finish of polishing furniture, mix turpentine with saw dust, and rub them well on the furniture.
- Rub your furniture with a mixture of olive oil and lemon juice to get a good shine, then polish with a soft, dry cloth.
- To remove tumbler ring marks on polished furniture, place a piece of blotting paper on it, and press with a slightly warm iron.
- To remove the ring marks of tumblers on a wooden surface, apply a little brasso on the stain. Leave for a few minutes. Then rub and polish with a soft rag.
- Mix olive oil and salt together, and spread it over the stained area of the wooden surface. Leave for about an hour. Then rub it with a clean cloth, and polish off the surface.

Glassware

- To add sparkle to your glassware, immerse it in water to which a little robin blue has been added. Then rinse with hot water.
- Use synthetic cloth to wipe dust from glass tops.
- It is easier to clean glass if a little borax is added to water.
- To give an extra sparkle to your glassware, wash in warm soap suds, rinse in cold water, then rinse in water to which is added a pinch of robin blue. Polish finally with tissue paper.
- To clean glass surface better, use a piece of nylon cloth as it attracts dust.

- For sparkling glassware, a few drops of ammonia added to the rinsing water will show good results.
- Apply a little toothpaste on glass articles and rub with a soft cloth. Any scratches on them will disappear.
- Stubborn stains on glasses can be removed with washing soda.
- Clean your glassware with water in which tea leaves have been boiled.
- Mix together tepid water with raw rice. Clean your cut glasses with this water. Rinse well in cold water, and wipe dry with a newspaper.
- Remove bulbs from their sockets. Wipe them with a piece of cotton moistened with methylated spirit. Dry well before replacing them in their sockets.
- You can clean your crystalware with vinegar-water solution.
- Mix together hot water and vinegar. Dip a thick wad of cotton in it and clean your chandeliers. Allow to dry.

Iron Articles

To remove rust from iron articles, apply a solution of lemon juice and salt.

Ivory

- Clean all ivory articles with a chamois cloth moistened with warm milk.
- Dip a small wad of cotton in alcohol, and wipe the ivory articles.
- To regain the whiteness of old ivory articles, cover them with a glass jar and keep them in the sun for a couple of hours.
- Dip a rag into a solution of borax and water, squeeze nearly dry, and rub the piano keys and ivory articles with it to get them gleaming.

Jewellery/Ornaments

- Soak a piece of cotton in methylated spirit and clean your diamond with it to give it extra sparkle.
- To bring back the sparkle to your oily, dull and dirty diamonds, soak them in half a litre of cold water to which is added three teaspoons of baking soda. Let it stand for four hours. Wipe dry with a soft cloth.
- Brush your diamond jewellery with a little toothpaste, then rinse them in clean water before wiping them dry with a soft cloth.
- Clean your diamond jewellery with a mixture of one teaspoon of detergent powder and one teaspoon of soda bicarb. Wash with an old brush and wipe with a piece of velvet cloth.
- To keep your diamonds glittering, soak them in four teaspoons of gin for half an hour. Rub dry with a soft chamois leather.
- Rub a piece of chalk on your diamonds. Clean with a soft, dry cloth. Your diamonds are now glittering.
- Clean your pearls with chamois leather.
- To clean pearl necklaces, place them in powdered magnesia. Brush off the surplus the next day.
- Apply oil on your coral ornaments, and let them dry for two days. They will regain their original colour and shine.
- After making paneer at home, soak your silver jewellery in the hot whey water. Leave it for a few minutes. Wash with soap and water. Wipe dry with a soft cloth to get them shining once again.
- A fine camel hairbrush dipped in eau-de-cologne will remove the dirt from the crevices of rings.
- Add a dash of ammonia to warm soapy water. Soak your gem-studded jewellery in it for five minutes. Then gently

scrub the stones with a small brush, rinse in cold water and wipe dry.

- To get your gold jewellery sparkling, wash them first in shampoo water, dry, then rub with a muslin cloth dipped in turmeric powder.
- Clean your gold jewellery with a solution of a pinch of baking soda mixed in detergent water.
- Soak your jewellery, that is dirty, in a solution of sodium bicarb, and leave for a couple of hours. Then wash with water and dry with a soft cloth.
- Soak your gold jewellery for an hour in a mixture of vinegar and turmeric. Then rub lightly with a brush, and wipe with a soft cloth.
- Immerse gold ornaments in sugar solution for some time. Then rub them with a soft cloth to give them a shine.
- Clean your costume jewellery with talcum powder, wipe with a soft cloth, then give it a coat of clear nail polish to prevent it from tarnish.
- Rub holy ash or 'vibhuti' over silver articles to make them glitter.
- Add a little milk to water. Soak your silver ornaments in this for 15 minutes. Rinse in clear water, and dry.
- Use the water in which potatoes are boiled to wash silver jewellery.
- Dip your gold and silver jewellery in hot shampoo water. Use a soft brush to remove the grime. Remove from the water, rinse in cold water, and wipe with a soft cloth.
- Place an aluminium foil in a large bowl, and put your silver ornaments in it. Sprinkle a teaspoon of baking soda over them, and pour hot boiling water over the lot. After 10 minutes, clean and wipe them. Your silver will be shining like new.

- Rub your gold-plated ornaments with pumpkin juice to make them shine.

Lacquerware
- Rub the lacquerware all over with gingelly oil. Leave on for a minute, then polish with a soft cloth. Give a final gloss to the articles by polishing with a dusting of dry flour and a fresh, soft rag.
- Clean lacquered brassware with spirit or vinegar, and wash off with water. Avoid using metal polish which corrodes lacquer work.

Laminates/Plastics
- To remove stains from your laminated surfaces, dip a cloth in lemon juice and rub the spot vigorously. Clean with a damp cloth and dry naturally.
- Rub olive oil on the laminated surface to remove stains and dirt. Wipe with a clean, soft cloth.
- For stubborn stains, make a thick paste with baking soda and water. Rub this mixture on the stain. Leave for two hours, and then wipe off. Finally apply a good wax polish.
- Dip a piece of small cloth in alcohol, and polish the plastic surfaces for a clean and shiny look.
- Rust marks on buckets and plastic tubs can be cleaned by scrubbing with turpentine to which table salt has been added.

Leather
- Rub petroleum on leather that has mildew on it.
- Mix two drops of camphor oil with two tablespoons of milk. Rub leather articles with this solution.
- To remove stains from leather articles, wipe with a piece of cloth soaked in warm milk. The result is immediate.

- To remove fungus from your leather goods, mix a little soda bicarb with milk, and clean them thoroughly. Then polish with a soft cloth soaked in lavender oil.
- To clean leather and give them an extra shine, rub with a soft cloth dipped in lemon juice.
- Wash chamois leathers in warm soapy water. Leave them with a lather of soap on them for 15 minute. Rinse, shake out the water, but don't wring them to remove the water. Leave them to dry away from direct heat. Once dry, crumple them up to bring back their softness.
- Wash your leather gloves with shampoo and water. Rinse thoroughly, and hang them outside in the shade. While still a little damp, put them back on your hands to help the gloves regain their shape. Rub together to soften them.
- For bringing back the shine to leather goods, rub a little Vaseline on them, and wipe with cotton.

Marble

- To remove stains on marble, rub with lemon juice, then rinse with plain water. When dry, polish with a good wax polish.
- Sprinkle some salt on a slice of lime. Rub the stained part on the marble top. Leave it for half an hour, then polish the surface with a clean cloth.
- While rust stains on marble can be removed by rubbing lemon juice, other stains can be removed with a paste of finely powdered chalk, pumice stone and common soda in equal parts. Rub this paste on the stain, and then wash with clean water.
- To keep the marble working counter in your kitchen clean, moisten a pumice stone, and gently rub over the discoloured area. Wash with soap and water.

- To remove lime stains or any other stains from kitchen counters made of marble or blackstone, apply some butter on the stains. Leave for a few hours, and then wipe with a clean cloth.

Mats/Mattresses

- To remove stains from mattresses and quilts, dry them in the sun. Apply starch paste on the stains and allow to dry well. Brush the starch off.
- To clean mats, rub them hard with coarse sandpaper, and they will be like new again.
- To keep rubber mat soft, soak it in a bath full of warm water. After an hour, rub the mat dry.
- To remove stains from cork mats, rub them with sandpaper. If the stains are damp, use a pumice stone instead. Remove the loose powder with a damp cloth, and then pat dry.
- To clear your coir door mats, place a newspaper under it. Stomp on them with your feet. Carefully remove the newspaper with the collected dust and dirt from the mat.

Metal

- To remove marks from chromium articles rub with a cut onion, and polish with a cloth.
- Vinegar and salt rubbed on the inside of copper boilers and such other articles will clean them and remove stains. Wipe with a damp cloth, and dry immediately with a dry cloth.
- If your copper or aluminium utensils get dark spots due to moisture during the monsoons, rub the spots with lemon or spirit.
- Put a few drops of cooking oil on a soft rag, and rub over bronze articles to clean them. Remove oil with a soft duster.

- Clean nickel fittings by rubbing them with cloth and some Vaseline. Wipe off with a little ammonia.
- An ink eraser or typewriter eraser can be effectively used for removing small spots of rust from metal.
- Boil an onion in a badly burnt aluminium pan. The burnt stuff will float on top.
- When aluminium vessels become dull or black, clean with cloth dipped in lime juice. Then rinse in warm water.
- To remove bad stains from the bottom of pans, mix together three parts of vinegar with one part of water, and simmer it in the pan for about 15 minutes. Remove, then boil an apple or orange in it for two minutes to bring back the shine to the tarnished pans.
- To remove the discolouration of aluminium pans, boil water with vegetable and fruit peels in them.

Mirrors

- Remove sticky labels on mirrors by rubbing them with alcohol or nail polish remover.
- Mix together powdered chalk and water or kerosene. Apply the mixture on the mirror and leave it to dry. Rub with a clean newspaper. Your mirror will be sparkling clean.
- To clean mirrors, rub with a damp newspaper roll. Use a little limestone before wiping it. It will give extra shine and leave no marks.
- Clean mirrors by rubbing them with a clean soft rag dipped in methylated spirit. Then polish with a soft dry cloth.
- Clean mirrors with water in which tea leaves have been boiled.
- To keep mirrors sparkling, apply a thin film of soap with moist fingers. Wipe and polish with a clean tissue.
- To clean a discoloured gilt mirror, rub over with warm turpentine mixed in hot water.

- Add a dash of ammonia to water, and rub the surface of the mirror. Dry and polish finally with tissue paper. The speckled stains will disappear.
- Remove fly-marks from mirrors by rubbing with a rag dipped in vinegar and salt. Polish with damp newspapers.

Ovens/Stoves

- To clean a greasy oven, put a little ammonia in a saucer and keep it inside the oven overnight. The ammonia fumes will work on the grease and it will come off easily the following morning.
- To clean discoloured gas fires, sprinkle generously with salt when the stove is not in use. When the gas is lighted, the salt will burn away, leaving the fire clean and without stains.
- Clean your gas stove with a mixture of vinegar and salt to keep it sparkling and insect free.
- Clean your gas stoves and kitchen slab surfaces with a mixture of equal quantities of coconut oil and kerosene, using a sponge.
- Bake an onion in the oven for about 20 minutes to remove food smell from it.
- To rustproof an old cake tin, wash and dry. Then smear it with lard and bake in a moderate oven for half an hour.
- To dispel smell in an oven, place several pieces of orange peel inside, and heat the oven on a low setting for 10 minutes.
- To wash very greasy or dirty cake tins, add some washing soda to boiling water. Use this water to wash and dry.

Paintings/Painted surfaces

- Clean oil paintings with a slice of potato. All the grime and dust will be removed to keep the painting clean and shining.

- Boil an onion in half a litre of water. Use this water to clean painted surfaces of all spots.
- Crayon marks on vinyl or painted surface can be removed with silver polish.
- After cleaning enamelled paint work, rub it over with a little furniture polish to give it a dust-resistant surface.

Sandalwood

To brighten items made of sandalwood, wipe it with a cloth dipped in milk.

Scissors/Knives

- Rub the handles of table knives with turpentine to keep them sparkling.
- Clean your scissors with a cut lime to remove the rust. Wipe with a clean cloth.
- Use water in which eggs have been boiled to clean dull cutlery.

Shoes/Chappals

- Leather shoes of any colour are best polished with petroleum jelly or castor oil, to keep them from drying and cracking.
- Paint your old pair of brown shoes with tincture of iodine. Clean in the usual way, and you will find them as good as new.
- To make the shoes shine brighter, add a little lemon juice to the shoe polish, and polish.
- Apply shoe polish and keep the shoes in sunlight for 15 minutes. Brush them again, and the shoes will sparkle as if new.
- Rub the inner portion of a banana peel on your leather shoes. Let it dry. Then brush them well. This cleans as well as conditions the leather.

- To retain the natural shine of leather shoes, and to prevent fungus formation, dip a small cotton wad in a little glycerine, and rub the shoes with it.
- Dried up and hard shoes or sandals can regain their original softness, by simply rubbing them with a piece of cloth moistened with glycerine.
- When leather shoes are scuffed and do not take polish, rub a cut potato on them before applying shoe polish. You will have shoes shining like new ones.
- Use a few drops of after-shave lotion to get rid of dirt from shoes, and to help restore the shine.
- If your leather shoes tend to look shabby, freshen them up by rubbing dry oatmeal with a soft flannel over them.
- To clean white shoes, simply rub them with a soft cloth dipped in nail polish remover.
- Always clean suede shoes with a rubber or bristle brush instead of a wire brush.
- To clean white sports shoes, wash them in soap water first. Then soak them in water to which a quarter teaspoon of citric acid is added. This will remove the most stubborn dirt from shoes, and leave them sparkling white.
- To condition leather shoes, rub baby oil into them and leave overnight. Rub off the oil in the morning.

Silverware

- To clean silverware, scrub them with a handful of hibiscus leaves and salt.
- Clean silverware by polishing with ordinary dry ash and common salt.
- To shine dull, stained silver articles, rub them with cotton soaked in methylated spirit.
- Use washing soda and alum in the ratio of 1 : 2 to clean silver.

- To give extra lustre to your silverware, clean with water in which potatoes have been boiled.
- To give a shine to your silver utensils, scrub them with rangoli powder, and then wash them with cold water.
- Ash from burnt paper can be used with advantage for cleaning silverware.
- A little milk added to the water in which silver is washed will help to keep it brighter.
- Make a thick paste of a tablespoon of turmeric powder and the same amount of detergent with water. Using an old toothbrush, apply this paste on your silverware. Rub hard for a few minutes before washing it away with warm water. The silverware will sparkle as new.
- Use toothpaste to polish on your silverware. Scrub with a soft and clean cloth.
- Rub a tablespoon of moistened cooking soda on the silverware to brighten them. Use a toothbrush on etched designs. Wash with water and dry well.

Spectacles/Sunglasses
- Remove all spots and grease from your spectacles by wiping with a soft cloth dabbed with eau-de-cologne.
- Clean your spectacles with a used tea bag. Dry off with a tissue for a sparkling effect.
- To clean the lenses of your sunglasses, use a drop of perfume on a clean tissue and polish well.
- Dab an old toothbrush with spirit and brush on your spectacles. Wipe with a soft cloth.

Stainless Steel
- Clean your stainless steel vessels with the residual coffee grains, after using its decoction, for a dazzling appearance.

- Remove oil stains from your greasy vessels by rubbing with used tea leaves.
- To remove a sticker label from a new vessel, fill the vessel with hot water, then remove the label. No marks will be left behind.
- Stains from stainless steel knives and plates can be removed by rubbing them with a cut potato.
- To keep your stainless steel glittering wash with tamarind juice.
- To remove stubborn stains from stainless steel, use a scouring pad dipped in a mild solution of ammonia and water.
- Use the whey water of curdled milk to clean your stainless steel water container for a clear and shiny effect.

Stationery

- Greasy smudges on paper can be removed if they are immediately liberally dusted with talcum powder, and vigorously rubbed, then excess powder dusted off.
- Rub a little wax in a thin layer on diaries and briefcases, and gently polish off. They will once again glisten.
- Clean rubbers or erasers on sandpaper.
- To clean an eraser, soak it in lukewarm water mixed with a little detergent powder. Rub the eraser a little and it will look new again.
- Use your hair dryer to clean the dust off your typewriters, computer keyboards and TV controls.

Suitcases

- Rub leather suitcases with a soft rag dipped in lemon juice to give an excellent shine.
- Rub a flannel dipped in a solution of vinegar and linseed oil on a leather suitcase, and wipe with a soft duster.

- To rejuvenate your worn-out-looking fibre suitcase, sponge it with warm water and vinegar. Finish off with wax polish and rubbing.
- To clean the rusty locks, chains or handles of your suitcase, rub with a piece of candle after rubbing the area with a cut lime and wiping it away with a clean cloth.
- To preserve leather suitcases from fungus and bad odour, keep a cake of soap in it.

Tennis Racquets

Clean tennis racquet guts with a sponge dipped in soap water, then in clean water. Wipe dry, and apply a thin layer of Vaseline to keep them from snapping.

Tiles

- Rub stained bathroom or kitchen tiles with a cut lemon. Leave it for 15 minutes, then wash.
- Rub sandpaper on bathroom tiles that have a hard-water coat. Clean with soapy sponge, then with clear water to restore their original shine.
- Clean bathroom tiles with a solution of salt and washing soda. Apply salt with a stiff brush on cracks between tiles. Allow to remain for ten minutes, then wash off with cold water.
- Remove rust stains from tiles with vinegar.
- Mix together four tablespoons of liquid ammonia with four and a half litres of water. Use this solution to wash the tiles in your bathroom.
- Wash ceramic tiles with a damp cloth dipped in methylated spirit.

Tyres

Wash the tyres of your car with cold water to double their lifespan.

Vases

To clean stains from glass vases, rub the stains with a solution of salt and vinegar.

Walls

- Use an eraser to clean dirty fingerprints off the walls.
- To remove marks from wallpaper, try rubbing with a soft India rubber, or with a small piece of stale bread.
- To clean and freshen ceramic-tiled walls, brush white shoe polish into the cracks around the tiles. Wipe polish streaks off the tiles with a dampened absorbent cloth.
- To remove moss on bathroom walls, use hot water and wipe.
- Wash dirty oil-paint walls with soapy water.

Windshields

Sprinkle a little baking soda on a damp sponge and clean your car's windshield, headlights and chrome accessories. Rinse with clear water.

Chapter Three
Domestic Tips

Aluminium
- Buy thick gauge aluminium vessels as they last a lifetime.
- Aluminium foil caps of used milk bottles can be used for scraping pans and griddles.

Balloons
Roll and stretch the balloons in your hands to loosen the plastic before blowing air into them.

Bathroom
- A rag soaked in perfume and kept in the bathroom will deodorise the place.
- Drop bits of old soap in your toilet cistern. When you flush your toilet, the melted soap cleans the toilet, and leaves behind a mild fragrance.
- To make your bathroom smell heavenly, fill the wash basin with water and add a few drops of eau-de-cologne. Let stand till you need the basin.

Belts
When making holes in leather or plastic belts, use a hot metal knitting needle. Heat the needle tip by holding it over a flame for nearly a minute, then pierce the hole in the belt.

Books

- To save rain-splattered books, put blotting papers on either side of the wet pages and keep the book under heavy pressure till properly dry.
- To safeguard books and paper against termites, wrap a few tobacco leaves in small open-mouthed cellophane satchets and place them inside each book.
- Rub a little colourless nail polish on the tear of a page on both sides. This is better than sticking a cellotape over it.
- Hang a small paper pad with a pencil at one side of your entrance to facilitate any visitor who calls in your absence to leave his/her name.
- A torn book page or currency note can be mended by painting it with the white of an egg and allowing it to dry.
- For book pages to retain their shine, sprinkle holy ash or 'vibhuti' in between them.

Bottles

- Drop a few drops of glycerine around the obstinate cork in a bottle. This will loosen the cork and it will come out effortlessly.
- Tight screw caps of bottles can be unscrewed by gently heating it, then twisting it open.
- To remove a stubborn cork, wrap a hot cloth around the neck of the bottle. Squeeze a few drops of ice water on the cork. The difference in the temperatures will loosen the cork.
- To open a new bottle, wash your hands with a washing soaps and wipe your hands with a dry towel. Now hold the bottle with one hand, and turn the lid with the other. The grip you get will be as firm as any plier.

- Rub your palm and fingers over a whitewashed wall. Now you can unscrew a stubborn cap on a bottle.
- Bottle caps that have got stuck can be coaxed with a lighted match run around the edges of the cap until it turns easily.
- You can cut bottles to any size or shape. Fill a bottle with water. Tie a twine, dipped in turpentine, over the area where you wish to cut the bottle. Light one end of the twine with a matchstick. The twine will burn slowly and the heat will cut the bottle at the required place.

Brooms/Mops
- To keep the broom tied tightly, add a teaspoon of fevicol to a teaspoon of water. Apply this to the handle of the broom. Secure it with a string which will remain tight as long as the broom lasts.
- After using a floor mop, rinse it thoroughly. Add several drops of household disinfectant to kill any lingering bacteria on it.

Brushes
- Don't discard old shaving brushes. They can be used for scrubbing dishes to a sparkle, using very little washing powder or soap solution. They last for ages, and your hands don't get affected.
- To soften paint brushes quickly, immerse them in hot vinegar.
- To make your new paint brush last longer, soak it in linseed oil for 12 hours.
- If a shoe brush is held in front of a heater and warmed for sometime before it is used, it will make the shoes shine better.
- Get a firmer grip on your paint brush by sticking a piece of foam around the handle.

- Remove all traces of paint from a brush by dipping it in white spirit.
- Cover the paint brush with kitchen foil, while pausing from a painting job, to keep the bristles soft.
- If your brushes have synthetic bristles, soak them in bleach for 15 minutes, and they will come out absolutely clean.

Camphor

To prevent camphor from evaporating put a few peppercorns in its container.

Candles

When there is a power cut, keep a candle in the bottom of a large basin with melted wax. Then pour some water into the basin. Now light the candle. If the candle topples over, there is no fear of anything catching fire.

Carpets

- When you want to keep your carpet rolled up, sprinkle a handful of fried chillies all over the carpet. Now roll the carpet, tie on the two ends with a large plastic sheet. This will keep away insects.
- When an old carpet or rug starts to curl up at the edges, coat the back with glue. Let it dry before replacing the carpet.

Cassettes

- Broken tapes from a cassette can be joined with a dab of nail polish. This will now sound as good as new.
- To keep your cassettes free of fungus, wind and rewind them three or four times fast.
- If your audio cassette is not working properly, having interruptions or low voice, keep it in the sunlight for a few days.

Chinaware

- To avoid breaking of fine china or glass while washing, place a thick Turkish towel at the bottom of the sink.
- Wrap breakable chinaware in damp newspaper when packing. When this dries, it will form a protective shell.
- Protect dinner plates by stacking them with a paper napkin on top of each plate.
- An old shaving brush washes ornamental china very well.

Cling Film

Prevent cling film from sticking to itself by storing it in the fridge.

Clock

If an alarm clock cannot wake the heaviest sleeper in your home, try putting it in a metal tin—it will magnify the sound.

Coconut Fibres/Shells

- Coconut fibres make an excellent scrubber for pots, pans and aluminium vessels.
- A coconut shell can be used as an ash-tray, a wall hanging, or for growing cactus. Rub the outer surface with emery paper to make it smooth.

Cord

A touch of clear nail varnish dabbed on either end of a decorative cord will prevent it from fraying.

Curtains

- Place used battery cells in the lower hem of the curtain to keep the curtain in place.
- To enable curtain rings to slide easily along the rod, apply paraffin to a cloth, and rub the rod briskly. Leave for a

while, and then polish with a warm, dry cloth before slipping on the rings.
- Curtains will glide along the rod easily if you spray the rod with some furniture polish.
- A small tear in a netted curtain can be fixed by applying some clear nail varnish.
- If you rub paraffin wax on curtain rods, the curtains will slide smoothly.
- To make netted curtains look crisp, dip the freshly washed net in a solution of one tablespoon sugar and half litre of water, and dry.
- Add methylated spirit to the water for giving a final rinse to lace curtains to make them soft and shining.

Containers

- If your container does not have an air-tight lid, smear a little oil near the opening of the container to prevent ants from getting into it.
- Soak a cloth in vinegar and rub it around the inside of a breadbox to prevent mildew forming. Dry well.
- To brighten up faded plastic containers spray paint first, then use fabric paints to make patterns on them in bright colours.

Cutlery/Scissors

- To prevent knives, which are used occasionally, from rusting, wash and dry after use. Rub over the surface with grease or Vaseline, and store wrapped in tissue paper.
- To sharpen scissors and nail-cutters, cut sand paper with them.
- By cutting a piece of glass with blunt scissors, the scissors will become sharp once again.

- To sharpen scissors, place the neck of a glass bottle between the blades. Trying to cut the bottle with the blades will sharpen them.
- To sharpen the knife blade, rub it on the underside of a china plate.
- Keep used blades separately in a wrapper. Use these blades after 15 days, and they are likely to give better results.
- Silver cutlery will remain clean longer if you wrap them up in cling film, after polishing them.
- Sharpen scissors by cutting across a metal knitting needle several times.

Doors/Windows

- Rub window panes with kerosene before painting window frames to prevent paint sticking to the glass.
- For a smooth movement of your sliding windows, rub the grooves with a candle.
- If doors and windows get jammed, rub a cake of soap along the edges.
- To prevent creaking of doors and windows, rub candles along the hinges.
- Prevent creaking of a door hinge by rubbing it with a lead pencil. The graphite in the pencil acts as a lubricant.
- Stop doors squeaking by spraying some washing liquid along the hinges.
- To stop windows misting up, wipe them with a cloth dipped in equal quantities of methylated spirit and glycerine.
- To prevent a car windscreen from freezing over on icy mornings, rub it over with a cut potato.
- Remove paint splashes from windows as soon as possible with turpentine. If dry, use a razor blade.

- To give a frosted look to a pane of glass temporarily, mix together two tablespoons of epsom salts with 125 ml of beer or brown vinegar. Dab mixture over the pane. Put on another coat, if necessary.
- If your door is creaking, rub a cake of soap on the hinges. Remove dirt with a toothbrush. Then rub Vaseline or sewing machine oil on the hinges.

Drawers

- Drawers that tend to stick will be much easier to open if you rub their sides with a candle.
- If a drawer squeaks, and does not slide with ease, rub a 5B or 6B lead pencil thickly along the sides. The graphite in the pencil acts as a lubricant.

Embroidery

- Before ironing a heavily embroidered cloth, lay a thick layer of soft material over the ironing board. Lay the embroidered cloth face down, and iron it. This will ensure that the raised surface of the embroidery does not get damaged or crushed.
- While embroidering any white fabric, apply some talcum powder on your palms to keep the cloth clean while you work.

Films

- Store films in the fridge, away from the back of the fridge where water might drip. Films last longer when stored at a low temperature.

Flasks

If you fill your thermos flask full, the heat lasts longer.

Furniture

- Before shifting furniture, fix bits of plaster to the base of the legs, for smooth sliding and to avoid scratch marks on the floor.
- Apply a coat of synthetic varnish on the lower ends of furniture legs. It will prevent erosion of polish and lustre, due to mopping the floor, in the long run.
- To darken wooden furniture apply a coat of beer. Let it dry, then apply polish.
- For easy gliding movement of heavy furniture on the floor, spread soap water on the floor where it stands. After moving the furniture, wipe it at once so that you don't slip on it.
- To cover up scratches or chips on your furniture, apply a thin paste of instant coffee and water. Leave it to dry. Seal it with a dab of clear nail polish.
- To move heavy furniture, sprinkle some talcum powder on the floor around the furniture.
- When the sun is beating down on your table through a window or door, cover it with a heavy blanket, or close the curtain, to protect the highly polished wood.
- While painting garden furniture outside, spread some sand or soil over the area. Any paint drips will fall on the sand or soil which can then be swept away.

Glassware

- If one glass sticks inside another, place them in the fridge and leave overnight. They will come apart without any problem.
- To release stuck glasses, put cold water in the inner glass, and hold the outer one in warm water. The inner glass will slide out soon enough.

- To retain the sparkle on the glass after washing and drying them, cover them with plastic bags before stacking them away.
- To protect glasses from breaking when moving house, pack them in bulb covers.
- To remove broken glass bits from the floor without pricking your fingers, run a handful of kneaded dough on them.
- To prevent milk glasses slipping from your children's hands, stick coloured sticking tape an inch below the rim.
- To pick up tiny pieces of broken glass, use damp cotton and brush over the floor.

Gloves

Dab a dash of enamel paint on the tips of the gloves from inside to prevent tearing of the gloves and breaking of nails while cleaning.

Incense

Incense sticks will burn longer if they are wrapped in a wet cloth for five minutes before lighting them.

Jars

To loosen a jar lid, apply a little cooking oil to which a pinch of salt has been added, and let stand for sometime before opening the jar.

Jewellery/Ornaments

- Keep Basra pearls in a container filled with basmati rice, to keep their lustre.
- For the corals to regain their original colour, apply oil on them and leave them to dry for two days.
- If your skin is sensitive to costume jewellery, coat the rear side of it with colourless nail polish.

- While putting on bangles which are tight, cover your hand with soap solution. The bangles will slip on easily.
- If you lose the screw of an earring, fix a small piece of rubber into the stem behind the lobe to hold the earring in place.
- If your gold chain is tangled up in a knot, dust it with talcum powder, and it will untangle easily.
- To prevent imitation gold jewellery from tarnishing, apply a coat of colourless nail polish on them.
- To retain the new look of artificial jewellery, keep them on a piece of cotton in a box with a piece of chalk in it.
- The metal chips on bow ties will never tarnish if you give it four coats of clear nail polish.
- To prevent glass bangles from breaking while putting them on, cover your hand with a nylon material and slip the bangles over it.
- To make glass bangles shinier, dip them in hot water, then soak in cold water for 15 minutes.
- To check whether pearls are real or not, put them in a glass of water. If they sink they are real.

Kettle

A piece of sponge placed inside a kettle will prevent it furring up if you live in a hard-water area. The scales will be drawn to the sponge instead of the sides of the kettle.

Keys/Locks

- If your key does not turn easily in a lock, rub a pencil point along the jagged edge.
- Use a pencil to lubricate door locks for easy opening and locking.

- To distinguish keys that look alike, dab on different nail polish on each, and likewise corresponding colours on locks.
- To release a jammed lock, cover the key with petroleum jelly, and move it around in the lock.

Lamps/Lampshades
- For maximum light efficiency, place lamps in the corner of the room to take the advantage of two walls to reflect light.
- Use old shaving brush for cleaning dust out of pleated lampshades.

Matches
Damp matches can be restored so that they light, by dipping the igniting end in nail varnish, and leaving them to dry.

Mattresses/Pillows
- When you go on a long vacation, place a few incense sticks under your mattresses to keep away creepy crawlies.
- The leftover pieces of cloth after stitching dresses, garments, etc., can be stuffed into a pillow cover, and the mouth of the pillow stitched. It makes for a nice and comfortable pillow.

Measuring Tape
Revive a limp measuring tape by ironing it between two waxed sheets of paper.

Mirrors
- Prevent the bathroom mirror from misting over by rubbing the mirror with a soft cloth dipped in vinegar.
- To stop the bathroom mirror from steaming up, wipe it over with shampoo, then polish with a clean cloth.

Nails/Screws/Hooks

- Dip nails in warm water before nailing them into the wall. The plaster of the wall will not come off while nailing.
- A couple of drops of ammonia will loosen up a rusty screw that refuses to come out.
- Before hammering a nail in the wall, apply a small cross patch of scotch tape over the spot to prevent the plaster from cracking.
- Dip the screw in thin paint and securely fix the screw on the wood or wall surface. This will also help to prevent rust.
- Apply coconut oil to the sharp end of iron nails before hammering them into wood or walls, and they will pierce in easily.
- Apply a few drops of vinegar on rusty screws and leave them to penetrate for a few minutes before using a screw driver.
- To prevent a screwdriver slipping, rub the blade with some chalk.
- Rub screws with some petroleum jelly before securing into place; this will make them easier to unscrew later.
- When tightening a loose screw, put some nail varnish under the head before screwing into place.
- Dip the nails in boiling water and then in molten wax or paraffin. They will then penetrate the wall easily.

Odours

- To remove the musty smells from rooms which are locked for a long time, burn camphor in the room for a couple of minutes.
- To counteract the smell of fresh paint, keep a bucket of water, containing several slices of onion overnight in the room.

- Leave a bowl of salt in a newly painted room to rid it of the smell of paint.
- In order to get rid of the musty smell emanating from books, dust them with talcum powder or powdered china-clay.
- After cooking fish, remove its odour from the pan by emptying tea leaves into it. Cover with water and leave for 10-15 minutes, then rinse and wash.
- To dispel the strong onion smell from a wooden chopping board, cover it with coarse salt, and then rinse under cold water.
- To remove onion smell from hands, rub a slice of lemon on your hands, and wash with soap and water.
- Lemon slices placed around a newly painted room will banish any paint smell.
- Scrub hands or vessels smelling of fish with a slice of lemon, then wash with soap and water.
- Put small bowls of vinegar around the room where smokers have congregated.
- Burning candle in the room cleans the air of cigarette smoke.
- To remove kerosene smell from your hands, rub a lemon peel well over your hands, then wash with soap and water.
- Wash vessels smelling of fish with vinegar.
- To rid your hands of onion smell, rub them with baking powder, and rinse.
- A bowl of white wine or vinegar placed next to the stove when you are frying, will cut down the smell and smoke. Place a bowl of it permanently near the stove; as the vinegar evaporates it deodorises the air.
- To dispel the burnt smell from the kitchen, boil a few pieces of lemon in a small saucepan.

- To dispel the burnt smell from the kitchen, boil a few pieces of lemon in a small saucepan.
- Boil cloves and cinnamon in a vessel to remove the smell of burnt food.
- When you burn a match in the toilet, the flame burns off the obnoxious gases, eliminating them immediately.
- To avoid the house smelling of boiled cabbage, place a crust of bread over the top of the cabbage while steaming it.
- While frying fish, put a slice of apple in the pan, thereby reducing the smell considerably.
- If your jar smells musty, fill it half with cold water, and add a tablespoon of dry mustard. Shake well and keep aside for half an hour. Wash and dry.
- Fill the musty-smelling jar with warm water. Add a teaspoon each of tea leaves and vinegar. Stand for three hours. Rinse and wipe dry.
- If your 'desi' ghee has a peculiar odour, just heat it and sprinkle some salt over it. Cool and use.
- To get rid of unpleasant shoe odours, put some fresh pine leaves inside the shoes.
- To remove the musty odour from an unused microwave oven, put two roses or used lemon rind into it, and run it for 40 seconds. It will smell fresh and clean.
- Rinsing cooking utensils in hot water to which salt has been added will keep them free of food odours.
- For odour-free drains, throw in a handful of baking soda in the drain, and follow it up with hot water.
- To prevent stale cigaratte smell from lingering in the room, put half a teaspoon of baking powder in the ashtray.
- To remove the odour of perspiration from clothes, dip them in water containing three aspirins.

Paint

- To remove paints from your hands, try using cooking oil instead of regular paint remover that often burns the skin.
- While storing a half-used tin of paint, replace the lid securely, and stand it upside down. This prevents the air from entering, and no wasteful skin will form on the paint.
- Remove old hard paint and varnish from old woodwork by softening it with liquid ammonia, and then scraping it off.
- To remove paint from your skin, apply curd on the affected part. After a few minutes, rub and wash it off.
- Rubbing petroleum jelly onto hands before painting makes it easier to remove any paint from them afterwards.
- Prevent a skin forming on gloss paint by pouring a thin layer of white spirit on top of the paint before replacing the lid.

Perfume

When your perfume bottle is empty, do not throw it away. Place it in between clothes with the lid open. Your clothes will be fragrant.

Plastic Bags

Store plastic bags in the freezer to stop them sticking together.

Playing Cards

To prevent the cards from sticking together, sprinkle some talcum powder over them. You will have a smooth deal!

Plunger

If you do not have a plunger at home, then use a thick sponge. This should have the same effect.

Polish

- If your boot polish dries up, add a few drops of olive oil or turpentine, or even alcohol or kerosene to soften it.
- Dip a cloth in petrol and rub the surface of a dry shoe polish, which can then be used to polish your shoes.
- Heat the old, dry and caked shoe polish in a tin container. Pour the melted polish into the original tin. Allow it to cool, and then use.
- If you have run out of brasso, dip a cloth in ketchup, and wipe the article to be polished with it. The brass will shine.

Posters/Pictures

- Use toothpaste to stick posters on walls. It does not damage the paint on the wall.
- When hanging pictures on the wall, place a drawing pin in each of the corners behind the frames so that air can circulate behind the pictures and insects will not breed there.

Pottery

When you notice a small chip in your white pottery, coat it with clear nail polish. This will prevent the porous clay from absorbing dust and stains.

Purse/Handbag

- While keeping away your purses and handbags when not in use for a long time, always stuff them with brown paper or tissue paper to retain their shape. Then put them in separate polythene bags.
- To bring shine to your leather purse, rub it with lemon peel.

Putty

Before applying putty on window frames, dip the knife into some clean water so as to prevent the putty from sticking to the knife.

Rangoli

Apply a thin paste of slightly heated maida-water solution on the ground or the base on which you intend to draw the rangoli. This way the rangoli will last longer.

Shoes

- Keep new shoes and chappals wrapped in a newspaper inside the cardboard box after every use.
- Stick a small piece of sponge on the inner surface of the shoe where it pinches.
- To avoid shoe bites, wear your shoes after wetting them and keep them on five hours. Your shoe will never pinch again.
- Apply a little mustard oil on the inner side of the shoe and leave it overnight. This will make the leather softer, and you will not have a shoe pinch.
- To avoid shoe bites, fill the new pair of leather shoes with soap solution, and keep for an hour. Empty the shoes, and dry under a fan.
- To avoid shoe bite, apply a little petroleum jelly on the inner side of the shoe.
- To ease tight shoes, keep a raw, sliced potato in the shoes overnight.
- Waterproof new leather shoes with linseed oil.
- To avoid shoe bite, just rub candle wax inside the shoe.
- To prevent children slipping with their new shoes on, stick a piece of sticking plaster on the soles of the shoes.

- To dry your shoes well, stuff them with newspapers which absorb moister better than cloth.
- Do not throw away your children's old canvas shoes if they are faded. Use your imagination and brighten them up with fabric colours.
- To avoid slipping with your new pair of leather shoes or chappals, sandpaper the soles a bit before you use them for the first time.
- After tying shoe laces, put a drop of water over the knot. The knot will not slip.

Washing, starching and drying Clothes

- Put used shampoo satchets in the washing machine during the wash cycle. Your clothes will smell good.
- Add a little vinegar to the water in which your soak coloured clothes are there. The colour will not run from any cloth.
- Add a little vinegar to the water for a final rinse of clothes to remove any soap traces from clothes.
- To brighten dull-looking clothes, soak them in hot water with a tablespoon of shampoo in it. Then wash as usual.
- To whiten dirty, stained white socks, boil them in water with a slice of lemon in it.
- To brighten old clothes, soak them in buttermilk for a day, and then wash.
- Add black ink to water while washing to brighten white clothes.
- Collect used lemon peels in a jar. Pressure cook and run them in a blender. Use a little of this while soaking white clothes in soapy water.
- Add a cup of turpentine to five litres of soapy water. Soak discoloured white linen in it for 12 hours. Then rinse in clear water.

- To remove excess dirt from clothes, add salt in the water in which you soak them.
- To make a bath towel softer, soak it in salted water for 12 hours.
- Apply a thick coat of talcum powder on shirt collar and cuffs, and leave overnight. Wash in the morning.
- Rub vinegar on stained clothes before washing.
- Soak shirt with a dirty collar in cold water. Rub a little sugar on the collar and keep aside for 10-15 minutes. Rinse in the usual way.
- To give a sparkling look to khadi clothes, soak them in a mixture of vinegar, gum and water for 10 minutes. Then spread them out without squeezing out the water.
- Soak dull white socks in water, which contains toothpaste, for 15 minutes. Wash with soap and water.
- If a coat collar is grubby, rub a dry pumice stone over it, then brush gently.
- To blue your clothes evenly, add salt to the blue water and rinse clothes in it.
- Add a little Robin Blue to the starch before starching dark coloured clothes.
- To stabilise the colour of a garment, soak it overnight in a solution of alum or salt in water.
- To retain the shine of silk materials, add two teaspoons of vinegar to the water while rinsing.
- Add a teaspoon of glycerine to a bucket of water and rinse silk saries to make them wrinkle free.
- To stiffen silk saries, soak them in cold water with a teaspoon of gum in it.
- To keep silk clothes shining squeeze half a lemon into a bucket of cold water, and rinse your silk in it.

- Organdie saris should not be starched, but ironed while still damp.
- Give your silk and woollen garments a final rinse in eucalyptus water.
- To protect the lustre of buttons, put a light coat of transparent nail polish over them before washing the garments.
- To make a new organdie sari drape well, soak it overnight in a bucket of water containing a cup of milk.
- While washing new woollens, put two tablespoons of ammonia in the first rinse, working up a good lather.
- To retain the texture and keep woollens from wrinkling, add a teaspoon of glycerine in the water while washing.
- To dry clothes in the rainy season, spread them on four layers of newspaper on the floor, and turn the fan to full speed.
- To avoid the strong smell of starch, add a little eau-de-cologne to the starch water.

Preserving and Storing Clothes

- Keep clothes stored with naphthalene balls.
- Keep pure silk and zari saris wrapped in tissue papers in the cupboard.
- Keep new incense sticks with clothes to keep away pests.
- Keep white or cream silk saris in blue tissue paper to prevent them turning yellow.
- Keep dried neem leaves instead of naphthalene balls with your clothes.
- Tie cloves in a netted cloth, and put them in between your silk or woollen clothes.
- Keep used mosquito repellent tablets among clothes to ward off insects.

- Keep empty soap wrappers or empty perfume bottles with lids off among clothes to keep away insects.
- Sprinkle sandalwood on brocades and silks to keep off moths and mildew.
- Fold cardigan properly, wrap it in an old towel with a few cloves, and insert it into a polythene bag.
- Place a new cake of soap amongst the woollens to keep them safe from insects.
- Wrap woollens in old newspapers, for the ink in them repels insects.
- Place camphor with four or five peppercorns among clothes. The strong smell of camphor will keep away insects, and the peppercorns will keep the camphor from evaporating.

Plastic Bags

Store plastic bags in the freezer to stop them sticking together.

Silverware

- Silver will not tarnish if you keep some camphor or alum with it.
- Put away unused silver in a box of flour to make it retain its brightness.
- Silverware should always be kept wrapped in tissue paper to prevent tarnishing and scratch marks.

Stamps

- To remove stamps from envelopes for philately, cut the paper on which the stamp is stuck. Keep it in a bowl of water for a few minutes, then peel off the stamp from the paper, and dry.
- To remove stamps stuck together, store them in the freezer for sometime.

Stationery

- If sketch pens go dry, open the sponge tube inside it, and see the change.
- To start your clogged ballpoint pen working again, insert the point in the filter end of the cigarette and give it a few quick twists.
- To use pencils which have become very small, insert them into the barrels of sketch pens that have become dry.
- Stick a small bit of sandpaper on the inside lid of your child's pencil box. It comes in handy for cleaning dirty erasers.
- A ballpoint pen that has stopped writing will write again if you rub the point on a glass surface.
- To stop a leak in your pen, rub the spot with a piece of soap.
- To prevent rubber bands from sticking in summer, sprinkle talcum powder in the polythene bag in which they are stored.
- To soften hardened glue, add some glycerine and warm water, and stir well.
- If your glue has become dry add a few drops of vinegar to it. It will become soft again.
- Stick a match to the end of a cellophane or scotch tape after using it. You won't have to hunt for the edge every time.
- When an end of a scotch tape sticks to the roll, just put it inside your fridge for ten minutes. You can now roll it out.
- It is easy to find the end of a scotch tape if it is dusted with talcum powder after use.

- The address written on an envelope with a marker or sketch pen will not wash away in the rains, if cellotape is stuck on the address.
- When mailing an envelope to a long distance destination, protect the label address by painting it over with colourless nail polish.
- To avoid the sticking of the envelope to the letter inside, keep a small piece of paper over the entire length of the envelope and then apply gum. Any gum oozing out will stick to the paper and keep the letter inside the envelope intact.
- Clear nail polish can often be substituted for glue to stick stamps or seal envelopes.
- To prevent addresses on letters and parcels running in wet weather, roll or rub a candle over the ink when it is dry.
- Add two-three teaspoons of water to your leftover fevicol tin, and fit the lid securely. The contents will remain good for use as long as you wish.
- To harden wax crayons, store them in the fridge overnight.
- When you lend your pen to someone, do not give its cap. The borrower of the pen will return your pen without the cap.

Steel Wool

To preserve steel wool and scouring pad from rusting, store them in a bowl or jar of water to which has been added a tablespoon of baking soda.

Tiles

When drilling into ceramic tiles, stick a bit of masking tape over the area. This will stop the drill bit from skating around.

Mark on the tape the required position of the hole, then drill the hole there.

Toolbox

- Place a few chalk bits in you toolbox. They will absorb the moisture and keep the tools rust-free.
- Place some camphor inside the toolbox to prevent the iron tools from becoming rusty.
- Keep a piece of charcoal in the toolbox. It will absorb water and avoid rusting of tools.

Venetian Blinds

- Wax or paraffin rubbed on the cords of venetian blinds make them last much longer.
- Wrap socks around your hands to facilitate the cleaning of each slat of the venetian blind.
- Wear old socks, one on either hand, while cleaning venetian blinds. Use one to wash, and the other to dry.

Walls

- For cracks on the wall, use toothpaste.
- To cover the hole left after removing a nail from the wall, stick a poster or a picture there.
- Crayon marks from a wall can be removed with a bit of toothpaste.

Wooden Surfaces

- To prevent disfiguring of wooden surfaces, frequently apply glycerine.
- Cover up screw holes in wood with a mixture of sawdust and adhesive. Once it is dry, sandpaper it and then paint it.

- While driving a nail into wood, apply paraffin wax to it for smooth penetration.

Zips
- The zips of purses, bags and pants will slide easily if you rub candles over them.
- If a zip fastener does not run smoothly shake some talcum powder over it, or run a pencil along its teeth.

Chapter Four
Sewing and Tailoring

- Coat your sewing machine bobbins with nail polish from the inside and outside to keep from rusting.
- Keep sewing needles in a box-filled with talcum powder to prevent their rusting.
- Soak rusty needles in kerosene for a day, then clean with a piece of cloth.
- When threading needles, dip the end of the thread in clear nail varnish. Within seconds you can easily thread the needle.
- Leftover bits of colour soaps can be used as marking chalk while cutting dark-coloured cloth.
- Hemline marks which are made while altering an outfit can be removed by rubbing the mark with a ball of cotton soaked in white vinegar.
- To cut thin slippery materials, dip the scissor blades in boiling water, wipe and use.
- If the knob of a knitting needle breaks, heat a small toothpaste cap until it melts. Ram the knitting needle into it and twist.
- Dust hands with talcum powder when knitting a sweater with white wool to clean it clean.

- After sewing buttons on a garment, apply a little clear nail polish on the threads at the centre of each button on both sides. The buttons will stay on much longer.
- Rub a wax candle across the teeth of a zip fastener on both sides several times to make the zip move easily.

Chapter Five
Gardening and Cut Flowers

Care of Plants
- Water in which eggs are boiled is good for plants.
- Rub each leaf of your indoor plant with any edible oil to make them shine.
- Weak tea is a good tonic for plants, and tea bags can be put in the pot.
- Use water in which pulses are sprouted for watering potted plants.
- Plant cuttings dipped in vinegar develop roots quickly.
- A weak solution of ammonia is good for plants.
- Onion peels put in with money plant will ensure its healthy growth.
- Scrape the stems of azaleas and asters to keep them better preserved.
- When plants are dying of worms, sprinkle dry mustard on top and put cold water to seep through. Worms will die or come up.
- Old aquarium water in which fish have been frozen makes an excellent fertiliser. Bring the water to room temperature first though.
- Add broken shells to the soil of your house plants, and see them bloom healthily.

- Once a fortnight mix a teaspoon of ammonia in a litre of water, and use it in watering ferns. This gives them a rich green foliage.
- Unused and expired medicines and syrups can be used as manure for plants.
- Used tea leaves make a very good fertiliser for rose plants.
- Plant four or five match sticks with the sulphur end down in plants infested with worms.
- Keep a few mint leaves in your potted plants that are kept outside, and no rats will approach these pots.

Preserving Flowers in Vases

- A little coconut oil applied to the edge of each petal of a rose put in a glass of water keeps the flower fresh.
- To preserve the freshness of cut flowers, burn the ends of the stalks before arranging them in a vase.
- To remove odour in flower vases, add a teaspoon of sugar to the water.
- Carnations last longer if they are put in a glass of water containing a little boric acid.
- Never place a flower arrangement where it will be directly exposed to wind from a fan, window or full sunlight.
- Add a few drops of cough syrup to revive withering roses, and trim the stems to increase absorption.
- Slightly slit the thick stem of a flower before placing it in a vase, for better water absorption.
- To add length to short-stemmed flowers, slip the stems into long straws before placing them in vases.
- Remove most of the leaves from the stems of flowers before placing the flowers in a vase. Foliage in water decomposes quickly.

- Add sugarcane juice to the water in the vase to keep flowers fresh for a long time.
- Add a little vinegar to a vase of flowers.
- Powdered aspirins lengthen the lives of freshly cut flowers.
- Ice cubes are said to be beneficial for flowers in vases.
- Keep copper coins in the vase in which you keep fresh flowers. This ensures a longer life for the flowers.
- Arrange flowers in porcelain or stone vases in summer for longer life.
- Use a syringe to spray water on flowers in a vase, morning and evening for longer life of flowers.
- Lay flowers that are to be arranged the next day in a vase, on a newspaper. Wrap them up with it and plunge the bunch of stems into tepid water.
- To keep a heavy flower from drooping, push a tooth pick through the centre of the flower into the stem.
- To keep flowers fresh longer, cut a bit of the stem each time you change the water in the vase.
- To freshen up artificial flowers, put them into a paper bag with a handful of salt, and shake well.

Chapter Six
Electrical Appliances

Batteries
- Batteries remain fresh if kept in the fridge.
- When torch battery cells go weak, they can be effectively recharged by drying them for a couple of days in the hot sun.
- To recharge your calculator cell, keep it in the sun for about 10 minutes.
- Keep the expensive battery from a camera in the butter compartment of your fridge, when not in use.
- Place old batteries in a standing position on top of the regulator of the fan when the fan is in use.

Bulbs
- To replace a burnt-out light bulb before it cools, insulate it with cover from the new bulb. Encased in the corrugated paper, the hot bulb can be unscrewed safely.
- Rub the light bulb with a cloth dipped in warm ammonia water.
- To remove the splintered base of a light bulb that has shattered in the socket, switch the power off at the mains. Then push in a cork, and twist anti-clockwise.

- Clean light bulbs with a piece of cotton moistened with methylated spirit. Dry well before replacing them in their sockets.
- Do not keep lamp holders empty. Always fix bulbs in them.

Electric Stove

Use wooden spoons for stirring when cooking on electric stoves, as there is less danger of shock.

Exhaust Fan

Make sure that you keep your exhaust fan clean and free of grease, else it will not work efficiently.

Fuse Box

- Keep a small card beside the fuse box indicating which light sockets are on which circuit.
- To test whether the fuse in your appliance has blown, open the battery compartment of a torch, and hold the fuse so that one end touches the end of the battery and the other end touches the terminal in the torch. Make sure that you are completing the circuit. Then switch the torch on. If the bulb burns, the fuse is all right.

Iron Box

- Brown marks on your iron box can be removed without scratching by rubbing them with a damp cloth and soda bicarb. Run iron over waxed paper.
- Heat the iron, and rub a candle over the spot where a material has stuck. The material will peel off automatically.
- Wet the surface of the iron. Rub an almond leaf over the spoilt area. The surface will become sparkling clean.
- To remove stains from your iron box, moisten a piece of cloth with vinegar. Rub the iron well with it.

- Rub the surface of the iron alternately with a muslin bag containing beeswax, and another one with salt. When the rust marks have gone, polish with a soft cloth.
- Place two sheets of aluminium foil between the ironing board and the cloth cover. As foil reflects heat, ironing is done twice as fast.
- Heat the iron. Remove the plug from the socket. Tie a piece of cotton material around a round-bladed knife, and gently scrape the surface of the iron with it to remove marks and dirt.
- Always use distilled water when filling a steam iron to prevent it furring up.
- Remove a sticky patch from the underside of an iron by gently heating it, switching off, and then running it back and forth across a piece of paper sprinkled with salt.
- If your iron box is not automatic, the electric coil may get burnt due to overheat. Keep switching it off frequently.
- To remove burn marks from an iron, rub lemon with salt on the iron when it is cold.

Kettle

- To remove fur from inside an electric kettle, fill it with a solution of vinegar and water. Boil it, then switch off. Leave for about six hours, then rinse thoroughly.
- When using the electric kettle, put off the switch when the water starts steaming out.

Mixies/Grinders

- If mixie blades are stiff, oil them to a smooth, working condition with a few drops of glycerine.
- Run a little dried bread in your mixie to remove the strong odour of spices, and to remove grease, if any.

- Before grating potatoes or cheese, grease the grater blade of the mixie with a little oil or butter. The job is less messy and there is no wastage.
- Run the mixie with some salt for a few seconds once a month. The mixie blades will be sharp.

Plugs / Sockets

- To prevent a plug from sticking in the socket, rub each of the pins with pencil lead.
- Keep all the sockets covered to prevent children putting their fingers in them, and also to keep them clean.
- Make sure you do not overload an electrical point with many electrical connections.
- For safety against electric shock or fire accident, use only three-pin plugs, and make sure the earthing is all right.

Refrigerators

- Keep all vegetables in the fridge in separate polythene or netted bags.
- Store green leafy vegetables in the fridge wrapped in a newspaper.
- Place a medium-sized sponge in the vegetable tray of the fridge. It will absorb the moisture and keep the vegetables fresh for a longer period of time.
- To keep vegetables in the fridge, line the tray with a small towel, and place another on top of the vegetables.
- When away on holiday, empty the fridge, and keep the door partially open to avoid the formation of fungus inside.
- Wipe smudge marks off your fridge with a little toothpaste dabbed on a sponge.
- Defrosting a freezer will be much easier if you rub the inside of the chamber with glycerine.

- To remove that yellowish coat from your refrigerator, mix a little soda bicarb and water. Apply a thin layer, and after five minutes, clean it with a wet cloth.
- When you go off on a long vacation, place two pieces of charcoal inside it, after defrosting and cleaning, to prevent fungus formation and bad odour.
- To reduce the load on the compressor of your fridge, use lightweight plastic plates or lids to cover food.
- Cut a lime in half, and place it in the fridge to keep the fridge free of odours.
- Keep a bunch of mint leaves in the fridge for your fridge to remain fresh and fragrant.
- A little vanilla poured on a piece of cotton and placed in the fridge will eliminate odours.
- An open box of baking soda inside the fridge will absorb food odours for a month.
- Mix equal quantities of salt and vinegar in a cup. Add a few drops of cologne in it to prevent your fridge from smelling.
- Brush the ice trays with a little oil or salt before putting them in the freezer. This prevents the trays from sticking to the freezer.
- After defrosting the fridge and cleaning out the freezing compartment, place trays on aluminium foil.
- Prevent ice trays from sticking by placing a sheet of wax paper under them in the freezer.
- Spray soda water on ice cubes to prevent them from sticking to the tray.
- Leave a few ice cubes in the tray and fill up the rest of the tray with water. Ice cubes will form faster.
- While storing a meat joint in the fridge, cover it with foil to prevent it from drying.

- Wrap meat in wax paper before storing in the fridge.
- When only some of the frozen food is needed, run very hot water over a sharp knife and cut the package in two. Wrap the extra portion in metal foil and quickly return it to the freezer.
- Apply a pinch of turmeric and salt to the fish if it is to be refrigerated for more than a day.
- Remove tops of root vegetable before storing them in the fridge.
- Peas keep better in the fridge when stored with their pods.
- Punch holes in polythene bags for storing vegetables in the fridge.
- It is best to turn the fridge to the coldest setting one-hour before freezing ice-cream, and then turn it back to normal setting.
- If your freeze is not full, fill empty plastic bottles half filled with water to fill up the spaces, for a full freezer functions more efficiently.
- Remove food stains inside with water and soda bicarb.
- Clean the fridge with warm water and soda bicarb.
- Keep a rubber mat in front of the fridge. If there is an electric shock while opening the fridge, the person will be saved if he stands on the rubber mat.
- Keep a few sheets of newspaper in the fridge to absorb extra moisture from vegetables.
- Add four teaspoons of mustard seeds in three-fourth cup of water. Keep it in the fridge to remove food odours.

Television
- Dab a little acetone on a cotton pad, and rub the TV screen with it to clean black spots. Wipe off with a soft damp cloth.

- If smoke emanates from the TV, the picture tube may have got burnt. Put off the power supply immediately to avoid short-circuiting and call for the TV mechanic to attend to it.
- A TV should be at least a foot away from the wall to allow sufficient air flow around it.

Toaster
- Sprinkle a teaspoon of salt on the non-stick toaster while it is still hot. Rub it with a ball of newspaper, or a soft muslin cloth. The salt absorbs the grease, and the toaster gets clean.
- Wipe the toaster with a soapy sponge. Then wipe with a soft and damp cloth.
- Mix together a teaspoon each of vinegar and lemon juice, and clean the toaster with it, using a soft sponge.
- Mix a tablespoon of soda bicarb and the juice of half a lemon. Smear the toaster with this paste. After a few minutes, rub off with a smooth muslin cloth. Clean it with a damp, soft cloth and dry again.

Vacuum cleaner
Coat the vacuum cleaner attachments with a thin layer of petroleum jelly. This makes it easier to attach and remove the parts.

Washing machine
1. To clean your washing machine of soap deposits and scum, fill the tub with hot water to which two cups of white vinegar has been added. Run the machine for eight to ten minutes. Drain and wipe dry.
2. Always close zips before putting the clothes in the washing machine so that they don't get damaged, and the zip is not caught in the machine rotator.

Wires / Cables

Use short lead wires to electric appliances. If the wire is long, the power losses are more.